"One of the most spiritual, yet realistic books of our time—they're phenomenal."

--Dr. Robert Carrol, Radiology Medicine

"Your books are very inspirational and provide the reader with gems of wisdom on how to pursue a more positive and harmonious life. They are truly remarkable."

--Anibal Acevedo Vila Governor, Commonwealth of Puerto Rico

"I have always taught my children to look on the bright side of life—and [your book] ATTITUDE expresses this concept perfectly."

--Bill Owens
Governor of Colorado, 1999-2007

"Thank you for your book on ATTITUDE. I'm adding it to my personal lending library at the office so my staff and others can read it, too."
--Jennifer Granholm, Governor of Michigan

"Ernie Carwile has a gift of integrating real life experiences and wonderful tales in a way only a master storyteller can do."

--Dr. James Gordon Emerson
Former President of the San Francisco
Theological Seminary

"As an avid reader in search of life's best, as well as a collector of inspirational quotes, I was enthralled with reading my first book in the Maxwell Winston Stone series...I not only highly recommend reading and rereading these books, but intend to purchase the series as gifts for all my loved ones."

--Cheryl Ellis, Allbrook Reviews

## ENDORSEMENTS AND PRAISE FOR THE MAXWELL WINSTON STONE BOOKS

"…Carwile's first novel should have a place in most book collections, with crossover appeal for readers who enjoyed Mitch Albom's *The Five People You Meet in Heaven.*

--THE LIBRARY JOURNAL

"Thank you very much for your book on "Attitude." It was 100% good stuff that we all need to absorb…"

--Steve Spurrier, Head Football Coach, University of South Carolina

"[In the hospital] the view for us all changes depending whether we are looking up from the gurney…or a doctor gazing down. THE MAXWELL WINSTON STONE series helps to remind us all of the journey and the big picture."

--Douglas V. Mayeda, MD, Diplomat of the American Board of Emergency Medicine

"These books speak to the world. Everyone should read them."

--Edwin Alexander, Former Director of the Federal Home Loan Bank

# THE MAGIC OF CREATIVITY

*Creativity is to Life as Spice is to Food!*

## ERNIE CARWILE

A MAXWELL WINSTON STONE SERIES

6

# THE MAGIC OF crEAtiViTy

Creativity is to Life as Spice is to Food

# Ernie Carwile

A Maxwell Winston Stone Series

Verbena Pond Publishing Co., L.L.C

For information, contact Verbena Pond Publishing Co.

at P.O. Box 370270, Denver, Colorado 80237

or call 303-641-8632.


ISBN: 978-0-9796176-5-2

Library of Congress Control Number: 2012954111

## DEDICATION

*To my Mary…sharing creativity with you*
*is one of my greatest joys.*

# OTHER BOOKS BY ERNIE CARWILE

*AND THE ANIMALS SHALL TEACH US: Angels in Disguise*

*ATTITUDE: It's Not What You See, It's How You See*

*CONNECTED BY THE SOUL: Oh, the Oneness of Us All*

*RECLAIMING THE POWER OF SILENCE*

*PERSISTENCE: The Art of Failing Until You Succeed*

*WHERE DO WE GO FROM HERE? Death, the Next Great Adventure*

*NEVER GOOD ENOUGH: Discover the Treasure of Self-Acceptance*

*CHIPPED BUT NOT BROKEN: When Adversity Enhances the Human Spirit*

*THE STORYTELLER 1*

# CONTENTS

# PROLOGUE

THERE HAVE BEEN MANY BOOKS WRIT-
ten on creativity. However, after reading a large
number of them, most seem to become bogged
down in the details, leaving me either confused
or frustrated. My goal here was to write a simple
book about creativity that everyone can easily
understand—where one can effortlessly grasp the
most important elements. But, more significantly,
this book was written to remind and encourage us
all to utilize creativity in our lives.

This book, like all the books in the MAXWELL
WINSTON STONE SERIES, is in a concentrated
form, meaning the information has been condensed
so you don't have to read a 300- to 400-page book
to glean the most pertinent information. As one
reader of the series so aptly described, "These
books are all meat; no filler."

*"Imagination is the preview of coming attractions."*

--Author unknown
(Often attributed to Albert Einsten)

*"Everything vanishes around me, and works are born as if out of a void. Ripe, graphic fruits fall off. My hand has become an obedient instrument of a remote will."*

--Paul Klee (1879-1940)
German Swiss Painter

# INTRODUCTION

*I REACH FOR MY PEN, THEN ADJUST MY writing paper with a slight shift to the left. Pausing to collect my thoughts, I tentatively begin to write. Choppy at first, I can see only fragments of thoughts, partially revealed ideas, but I press on.*

*Then, something happens of which I am only vaguely aware; an invisible Source connects with my mind and words begin to flow. I know not from whence it came; only that it inhabits me, and I soon find that my hand seems to be moving involuntarily, somehow now connected with the Source as it filters through my mind.*

*It is then I depart from this world and enter a new dimension that is infinitely better than where I was. Though I realize I am a mere vessel through which the Source provides, there still resides a pride more profound than if the writing had originated from me.*

*The muscles in my hand and wrist threaten to convulse, freeze up from the continuous exertion, but I can no more stop the flow than I could halt a speeding train.*

*In this moment, this sacred frame of reference, I find something more satisfying than even fame and fortune; something near ecstasy, but calmer and more enriching than normal life. This is what is meant to be creative, to be ensconced in a creative state, to be transformed, to hear and receive beyond normal organ hearing, acute receptivity that exceeds the boundaries of rationality.*

*Is this why we are created I wonder — to create? Certainly most of our day-to-day lives seldom approach such richness. If, in this state, I have stumbled upon the meaning of life, than I stand in awe, in reverence, for I have entered into the holy.*

✳ ✳ ✳

This is the ninth book in the MAXWELL WINSTON STONE SERIES, and if after reading the above you are thinking, "Oh, this book isn't for me. I'm just not a creative person," let me say that this book is ***especially*** for you, along with all the other people who already realize they can be creative.

You do not have to be a sculptor, painter, actor, dancer, or a musician to utilize creativity, for it can be used in *every* aspect of your life. Creativity and imagination (I use these words synonymously) can and will transform your life.

Do you really believe you are not creative?

Remember as a child when you tied a towel around your neck—a magic towel that you colored with a large "S"—and suddenly you were Superman; when a pair of shoes you believed were made of glass transformed you into Cinderella; or when, by clicking the heels of your shoes together, you could spend your entire day in Oz? This is what I'm talking about. This is creativity.

Unfortunately, as we age, often that spark—your spark—is diminished. My hope is that you can rediscover it and enrich your life in ways never before imagined.

Where some people *eat to live*, I *live to eat*. Sitting down to a five-course meal with all the wonderful flavors and smells that accompany it is truly one of my greatest pleasures; though make no mistake, I love chomping down on a delicious hot dog, too. But to bite down on something with zero flavors is not only a disappointment; it is a complete waste of my time and certainly not worth the calories. See, it's the *seasonings* that make the difference.

This is what I mean by, "Creativity is to life as spice is to food," for without *spice* (or *creativity*), your life will be as boring as a potato without butter and sour cream, a hot dog without mustard, or a life without passion and joy. It's as simple as that.

Come with me now as we enter into a *magical space* called *creativity*, that sacred place inside each of us...where our lives can be transformed to do the seemingly impossible.

*"The flipside of boredom is creativity."*

--Maxwell Winston Stone

# CHAPTER 1
## THE GENIUS IN US ALL

*"A bird doesn't sing
because it has an answer;
a bird sings because it has a song."*

--Lou Holtz Retired American football coach,
active sportscaster and motivational speaker

ARE YOU HAPPY AND FULFILLED IN YOUR life? Or, are you feeling stuck and bored, believing there is nowhere to go?

What if you were not supposed to be a bird in a cage, but rather, an eagle soaring in the sky? What song is in your heart waiting to be sung?

Or, as a team member of a company, what if you were provided an environment which enabled you to tap into revolutionary ways to market your product...a creative new paradigm of marketing never before utilized...so different, so unique, so surprisingly successful that a few years into the future your company would look back and wonder why no one had thought of it before? Would you like to be able to predict the future as to the new directions your company will be taking...new products and old product redevelopments?

How about if you are in school...would you like to be perceived by the teachers and the school system as someone really bright?

Can you grasp that what you need is a change in your thinking to allow creativity to provide you with a plethora of new options? See, changing your thoughts is as easy as using creativity. By opening your mind to new ways of thinking you open the universe to a menu of new and exciting ways to live.

"Oh," that little voice in your head might be whispering, "I could never do to those things...I mean, I'm no genius." Right?

Wrong. Let me share with you some startling new discoveries pointing to the truth, the reality that **every person has a genius residing within them** waiting to be developed or unleashed. And make no doubt about it; I am using the term genius literally and with no excessive embellishment whatsoever.

In researching this truly startling new idea, I discovered a false belief I had been holding onto— the belief that intelligence, as measured by I.Q. scoring, was fixed, meaning that a person's I.Q. was set in stone and could never be increased. Initially, this breakthrough came after accidently stumbling upon a quote by Alfred Benet, the inventor of the original I.Q. test back in 1905. He said, "Some recent philosophers seem to have given their moral approval to the **deplorable verdicts** that affirm that the intelligence of an individual is a fixed quantity, a quantity that cannot be augmented. **We must protest and react against this brutal pessimism; we will try to demonstrate that it is founded on nothing.**"

Once again, I discovered another false myth, a lie that I had somehow grown up believing, that no matter how hard I tried to be smarter or a better athlete, or if I attempted to create something new and beneficial for our world, my talents and abilities would always be *capped* by an I. Q. bestowed upon me from birth!

My next insightful discovery, shattering this limiting false idea, came when I came across two little books: ***THINK LIKE A GENIUS*** by Todd Siler; and ***THE GENIUS IN US ALL*** by David Shenk. After reading each book, I immediately concluded that every kid and adult should read these books. Why? Because they provided not only hope, but actual scientific substantiation that we are not limited in any way resulting from an initial I.Q. test, berating parental influence, nor biased teacher evaluations.

Here are some of the revelatory discoveries I gained from the writings:

- Everyone's brain has the capability to become almost anything we demand from it;
- Everyone can grow smarter if the environment demands it;
- Where everyone is born with differences and some are given special or unique advantages, no one is genetically designed into greatness and few are limited, biologically, from attaining it.;
- I especially loved this one—different genes simply make us people who possess different abilities. Someone one once said that everyone may truly be a genius. However, if you judge a fish by its ability to fly, the poor fish will live its whole life believing it is stupid;
- I garnered from their collective ideas that our world does not have a scarcity of talent, but in actuality a great abundance of *latent* talent that has not yet emerged;

- Finally, I definitely learned that our abilities are not set in stone and that greatness, however you define it, is something any adult or kid can truly aspire.

With this new beautiful input, can you imagine how a kid who has already been labeled slow by their teachers and our educational system, and/or even a kid who was a troublemaker because of his own feelings of inadequacy, might now react to this new understanding? Why, he might come to understand that by using his own imagination, a talent he has already been using, though often in negative ways, may now be used to actually enhance his I.Q—to disprove his teachers and everyone else who thought he was dumb and a loser.

Or what about you and me? Can you imagine how we, with our own feelings of inadequacy and low self-worth, might now react with this transformative input?

Using creativity is certainly **one of the ways** in which we can unleash our genius power. Could it be one of the keys you had somehow been hoping to discover that would allow you to be the genius *you* had always secretly hoped, suspected?

\* \* \*

A moving story about Abraham Lincoln comes to mind about how his creative handling of an extremely difficult situation diffused an embarrassing and painful moment. The story goes that after the Civil War had concluded and the North was celebrating its victory over the South at a huge ceremony, General Lee, the proud commander of the South, was sitting uncomfortably and obviously embarrassed to be at the surrendering ceremony.

During the rather raucous ceremony, the band leader continued to ask President Lincoln when he wanted the "Battle Hymn of the Republic" to be played. Lincoln kept deferring, as he watched General Lee trying to keep his composure, all the while thinking of the many young men who had died in the war.

It was then that President Lincoln shocked the band leader by informing him he did not want the "Battle Hymn of the Republic" played, but instead he requested that they play "Dixie." The crowd was confused as the band played out the words, "Oh I wish I were in the land of cotton…"

The audience, made up almost entirely of Northerners, sat initially stunned by the song. Silence enveloped the crowd. But by the end, and with the words echoing, "In Dixieland I take my stand to live and die in Dixie…," there was not a dry eye in the crowd. True healing began for our country at that moment.

A complex dilemma or a simple one, creativity can always provide us with a solution.

*"It is better to create than to learn!
Creating is the essence of life."*

--Julius Caesar (100 BC-44 BC)
Roman General and Statesman

# CHAPTER 2
## WHAT IT IS

*DO YOU KNOW WHAT COLOR IS MOST conducive to providing a creative environment? Would you like to know which it is?*

*Did you know that the "old brainstorming" technique is no longer the optimum way to generate the most and best creative ideas? Want to know what is the new method?*

✳ ✳ ✳

Interestingly, I could not find a common definition for the word *creativity*. Combining the best of the best, here's what I came up with to define this process: **Creativity is the ability to transcend traditional ideas, roles, patterns, and relationships by creating new ones; it is a process of arriving at new, unique, and uncommon ideas; it is a method of thinking which utilizes non-logical thinking that is characterized by innovation, originality, and risk-taking.**

Whether you believe it or not, creativity is *innate* within everyone. It can be used in every facet of living. Here is a fable about how a desperate businessman used it to save his family's business.

*A Chinese family owned a store in Manhattan. The store had been in their family for three generations, and the father anticipated bestowing it upon his son when he retired, as his father had before him.*

*One day a very prosperous, well-dressed man entered the store and explained he was a developer who had purchased the entire block where the Chinese store was located. He further explained how he was going to erect a huge mall and needed only their small store to complete the project.*

*When he offered the Chinese man a very good price for his shop, the owner humbly explained that because the shop had been in their family for three generations, it was not for sale. He further explained that he planned to give it to his son when he retired.*

*Well, the rich developer made another offer, then another even higher, while the Chinese man continued to politely turn down each one.*

*Angrily, the developer left the store and returned to his office where he called all of his brightest employees together. "Look," he said, "this little twerp thinks he's going to prevent me from completing my mall and we're not going to let him. I want us to think and come up with a way to put this guy out of business."*

After exchanging ideas, they eventually arrived at a fabulous solution. What they would do at the "grand opening" was hang two huge banners, one on either side of the little store's door that said, "GRAND OPENING."

Now when the Chinese store owner saw their signs, he was crushed. Calling his family together, he explained what the rich mall owner had done and sadly confessed that they might very well be put out of business.

It was then the oldest son spoke up and proposed that they needed to find a creative way to overcome the signs; so they did.

Their solution was to purchase a large sign themselves. Remember that the developer had hung the two large signs on each side of the little store's doorway announcing, "GRAND OPENING."

Guess what the Chinese family did? They hung their own sign over their store's entrance way between the "Grand Opening" signs. It read…**"MAIN ENTRANCE."**

They quadrupled their yearly sales during

*the first two weeks!*

What about using creativity in business relationships? Here's an example:

*In the produce section of a large grocery store, the assistant manager noticed that one lady looked perplexed after she picked up a large grapefruit.*

*Walking over to her, he asked if there was a problem, to which she replied, "This grapefruit is too large. I need only half of it but can't find the price for half a grapefruit." The young assistant manager smiled sagely and said, "I'm so sorry, madam, but we don't sell grapefruits by the half. (This took place quite a few years ago, before grocery stores did this.)*

*Well, the lady became irate and began objecting to this policy. In response, the young man told her to wait a minute while he went to speak with his manager.*

*When the young man entered his manager's office, he explained to him that this "lady" was complaining about the store's policy of not selling grapefruit by the halves. What he didn't know was that the lady had followed him into the manager's office and heard him tell his side of the story.*

*Suddenly, seeing the lady behind him, he thought for a second before adding, "And this nice lady said she would take the other half."*

*After the now satisfied lady left, the impressed manager asked the young lad to sit down and congratulated him on how he'd handled this potentially explosive situation quite creatively. He next asked where the young man was from. Proud that the manager had singled him out and anxious to please him with a bright response, he said, "I'm from Baltimore, sir, where they have a great football team, but ugly women."*

*The manger's face dropped and the room's temperature became much cooler. He replied, "Young man, my wife is from Baltimore." To which, after silently berating himself for the huge faux pas, the assistant manager paused, gathered his wits, and said meekly, "What position did she play?"*

These are just two fun ways where creative thinking turned challenging life situations into positive results. The lesson to be learned and never forgotten is: CREATIVITY MAY PROVIDE A SOLUTION TO EVERY CONCEIVABLE

PROBLEM THE WORLD THROWS AT US.

The Source from which creativity originates and flows has been called many different names: If you are a professor of English, you might call it the "muse"; a psychotherapist would say "stream of consciousness"; a Christian, "God or Christ"; a non-religious but spiritual person might say "Creative Universe." The point is that whatever you may call it, *something* really is there; some force or power or source of knowledge is simply waiting for us to call upon it.

Something happens in our brains when we enter into a creative state, something that feels so different from our normal state of being and enables us to tap into a reservoir of wisdom and knowledge that is always available. How? By going to the part of our brain that deals with creativity and imagination, just like other geniuses have done.

Creativity can be used in whatever dilemma confronts you, whether complex or simple, like in this story:

*Growing up in a pioneer community during the late 1800's, the main center of social life was the church, and Sunday meetings were always the highlight of each week. This was* the time when neighbors from the surrounding valley came together and created a community consciousness. It was also a time for the best manners and best clothes, when everyone tried to impress one another.

A new farming family moved into the valley, and feeling a bit shy, the father had made arrangements to stop by their closest neighbors to ride together into town and help break the ice for their first Sunday.

When the new family—the father, mother and young daughter—rode up to their neighbor's home, the family's daughters were horrified to see that the new woman and her daughter were wearing aprons to church. This was a real faux pas and the older girls knew the new family would be victims of certain ridicule as a result of this breach of etiquette.

The girls' mother, seeing her daughters' reaction to the new mother and daughter's aprons, quickly excused herself along with her two daughters and went back into the house. Emerging moments later with smiles and greetings, they climbed into the wagon to accompany their new neighbors to Sunday meeting.

*You see, all three women had put on their aprons to match the newcomers!*

All you have to do to be creative is simply be aware that a problem exists and then search for the optimum solution. It is truly as simple as that.

**I repeat:** *for every problem, there exists a solution that may be discovered through creativity.*

*"I saw an angel in the marble and carved until I set it free."*

--Michelangelo (1475-1564)
Sculptor, Painter and Architect

# CHAPTER 3
## HOW WE LOST IT

I FIND IT INTERESTING TO OBSERVE THE faces of people when I am speaking about creativity. When I first mention the word—creativity—some of the faces in the audience light up while others stay neutral. With some, I swear I see invisible "ear plugs" and "eye blinders" magically appear. I can almost read their minds as they internally repeat, *"I am not a creative type of person and never will be."*

What saddens me when I see or hear this is that every one of us is creative, whether we know it or not. We are all born with a natural, innate ability to be creative. Along the way, something or someone convinced us that we weren't…and we believed it.

Do you remember a man named Leo Buscaglia?

*He was an associate professor at the University of Southern California. While teaching a class, he heard that one of his students had committed suicide. Powerfully moved by the incident, he altered his teaching agenda to include a class on "Love," which later brought about his moniker, "Dr. Love."*

*Leo Buscaglia strongly believed in the absolute importance of creativity and continually urged others to use it in their lives. In offering one explanation as to why many people believe they are not creative, he told a story that went something like this:*

*It was in a kindergarten class where the teacher announced that today they would be drawing a picture. One little boy named Patrick was especially excited about this, as he was an artist from way back. The teacher handed out blank sheets of paper and brand new boxes of crayons. Remember them? Remember how they smelled? Each box was filled with exotic colors, and since the box had been unopened, each of the crayons still had pointed tips, which made for easier coloring.*

*On this day, the teacher announced they would be drawing a tree. Patrick beamed brightly, for he had already drawn many other things, such as lions and tigers and flowers, and knew that a tree would be a breeze to draw.*

*Studying all of the crayon's colors, he finally decided on the color purple to use for the tree's trunk. He didn't want his tree to be just any tree, so with great skill he colored in a tree with a magnificent purple trunk.*

*Then, for the leaves, he employed such bright and beautiful colors as green and orange and yellow and red. Smiling proudly at his creation, he could hardly wait for his teacher's approval. But when the teacher saw his drawing, rather than compliment him on his creativity, she chastised him by pointing out that trees have brown trunks and green leaves. She then told him to draw a "real tree."*

*Patrick was quite disappointed over his teacher's rejection of his creation but took in a deep breath, let it out slowly, and pulled out a clean sheet of paper.*

*Trying to heed his teacher's instructions, he reached for the brown crayon and carefully drew a brown tree trunk. But something happened to him as he was reaching for the color green. You see, something inside him wouldn't let him just draw a normal, dull tree with green leaves. So, this time he chose the unusual colors of fuchsia, chartreuse, lavender, lime, and emerald. This resulted in an extraordinarily beautiful tree. He was certain the teacher would <u>have</u> to praise him for his artistic creativity.*

*You may have already guessed what*

*happened. Once again, the teacher berated him for not drawing a "real tree" and told him for the second time to do it right.*

*So, little Patrick pulled out a new sheet of paper, drew a tree with a brown trunk and green leaves…and never tried to be creative ever again.*

Can you relate to this story? You can't believe how many people come up to me and tell me variations of this story from their own personal life experiences. Can you think of personal examples that demonstrate how YOU lost this inner ability? Somehow it must have been stifled within you or you would already be using it in every area of your life.

Another illustration that brilliantly depicts how many people lose or give up their creative urges came about in an ad by a now defunct corporation. On one of their advertisements, they had drawn nine boxes, three to a row. In each box was a statement followed by a picture of a light bulb. In the first box, the statement said "I have an idea," which was followed by a picture of a light bulb emitting a great amount of light.

The next box held the statement, "A word of caution," and you saw that the light bulb diminished in brightness. These comments were followed by other statements, such as, "A little too radical for us," "I like it myself, but...," We tried something like that once...," "It's not just us...," and "I wish it were that easy." My personal favorite negative comment was, "Let me play devil's advocate." Of course, with each comment, the light bulb continued to diminish until in the last box, the comment stated, "Oh, it was just an idea," and the light bulb went out completely. This is what so often happens to our creative ideas.

I've been told by many educators that sometime around the fourth grade kids develop an "inhibiting mechanism," because of their compelling desire to *fit in* and not be seen as different. Thus, in their desire not to stand out, to be a part of the group, they choose to withhold their creative insights that would reveal their uniqueness and individuality to the group.

Leaders of organizations may say they want creative ideas, but in actuality, reject creativity in favor of *conformity and uniformity.* It has also been proven through blind studies that many primary school teachers liked the creative kids *least.*

Someone once said that all children start out as artists, but the key is how to retain this ability into adulthood.

\* \* \*

*Lest you think I forgot, the color that provides the best environment for us to be our optimum creative selves is—BLUE. The reason for this is that blue reminds us of the open sky, sandy beaches, blue ocean, and those lazy, crazy days of summer. This color allows us to feel safe and therefore more creative.*

*The question as to why the "old brainstorming" method is no longer the most effective way to generate fresh new ideas will be answered shortly in an upcoming chapter.*

*"OUR CREATOR
       CREATED US
              TO CREATE"*

--Maxwell Winston Stone

# CHAPTER 4
## WHERE IT'S LOCATED
## IN THE BRAIN

OUR BRAINS CONSIST OF TWO HEMI-spheres: the left and right sides. Whether we are aware of it or not, when we are being creative, we are in the right side of our brain, not the left. You may already be aware of the characteristics that are in each hemisphere; but it would be beneficial to have a quick refresher.

The **left-brain** characteristics are:
- Used most in our everyday living;
- Our logical thinking side;
- Linear thinking;
- Rationality;
- The part that says, "I am," which is good, but it separates us from one another;
- The part that deals with the *past* and the *future*; and,
- Analytical.

The **right-brain** characteristics are:
- Our intuitive sides;

- Living in the present;
- Our feelings;
- Interconnectedness with all living things;
- Holistic perspective; and,
- Spirituality.

Remember these characteristics. Learn them because they will help you better understand the creative process.

And just so there is no misunderstanding, we need *both* sides of our brains to function in our daily lives. Being Spock on *Star Trek* and believing logic was the optimum key is actually not the highest mental state; we need both sides of our brains for different functions.

Even in problem-solving, logic *can* solve a great many problems; but when we are faced with a problem that logic cannot solve, we simply need to learn to shift to the right brain, just as other geniuses have done to make their amazing discoveries. Just like them, for us to solve the difficult problems that confront us, whether in business, relationships, cooking, furniture and flower arranging, acting, painting, or writing, the right brain is key.

You'll soon read more about how you can learn to shift from the left to the right side whenever you wish to do so. But oftentimes, you may not even be aware that the shift has taken place. It's like going camping on a day when it has rained. Frustrated that you can't find any dry wood to start a fire, you suddenly realize the pine trees surrounding you have probably protected the fallen tree limbs below them. There, you discover plenty of dry wood.

This idea most likely came from an *intuitive insight*, a mysterious event that occurs in the brain and brings about a solution. You can call this imagination or creativity, but whatever term you wish to use, it is something that is very real and always available.

*"Science does not know its debt to imagination."*

--Ralph Waldo Emerson (1803-1882)
American Essayist and Poet

# CHAPTER 5
## A MOST INCREDIBLE STORY

LIKE YOU, I RECEIVE WAY TOO MANY emails that are a waste of my time, and I spend a fair amount of additional time trying to limit incoming emails to only those that might be enlightening or personal.

But, without a doubt, one of the most fascinating emails I've ever received was about a lady named Dr. Jill Bolte Taylor. Partially because of having a brother who suffers from the brain disorder of schizophrenia, she devoted her life to studying the brain and often worked with *stroke victims*. In her own words, she admitted that she pretty much stayed in the left side of her brain, the rational side, in trying to better understand the workings of the mind.

You've no doubt heard the word "ironic," which is when the end result of something is the opposite from what was expected. Irony occurred to Dr. Taylor, when she awoke one morning with a dull ache in her head. Having worked primarily in her left brain—trying to help stroke victims—

she shockingly realized *she* was in the midst of a stroke that morning when she found herself initially unable to move or talk.

Even more ironic was the fact that this stroke shut down her left brain, the side where she spent most of her waking life, leaving her totally trapped in her right brain. This should have been exceptionally frightening, right? Yet, here's what she discovered:

- In her right brain, she found feelings of deep inner peace;
- Her right brain held the expressions of peace, love, joy, and compassion;
- This is the place where we have our mystical experiences;
- Her right brain was adventurous and celebrated life's abundances;
- Her right brain was socially adept, sensitive to non-verbal communication, and accurately decoded emotions;
- It's the place where we live in the present;
- It was here that she felt *at one with the universe*;
- Her right brain was the seat of her divine mind, the source of her intuition and higher consciousness.

She best described her overall feeling about

being "trapped" in her right brain with these words, "It is so cool here. I feel I'm in nirvana."

Perhaps this story might provide you with a better understanding of just how wonderful being in the creative state can be. It might motivate you to enter into this frame of mind more frequently. Also, if you wish to read more about Jill's amazing story, her book is entitled *My Stroke of Insight*.

This story is extremely powerful because it opens up and enlightens us about this right side of our brain, this mysterious area that until recently many people remained ignorant of and skeptical about. This is strange because, at least as children, we openly used it every day.

We live in a grand age and with our new understanding of creativity and imagination, we can now become the **great problem solvers** in our world's evolution. Truly, today we are coming to believe that we can solve any problem that confronts us.

*"Three steps for solving any problem:*
*1. Utilize Creativity;*
*2. Be Persistent; and,*
*3. Take Action."*

--Maxwell Winston Stone

# CHAPTER 6
## TECHNIQUES FOR SHIFTING

THE GOOD NEWS HERE IS THAT WE DON'T need to have a stroke to shift to our right brain. In fact, we can accomplish this any time we desire. Where there are an infinite number of techniques people have either consciously or unconsciously utilized in bringing about this shift, here are some of the most common and interesting to me:

- Prayer and Meditation. This is, by far, the method most used. It is the one I often incorporate into my creative life.

- The famous and most influential psychiatrist, Carl Jung, when unable to find a solution to a patient's problem, would go down to the river and "stack rocks." This simple process somehow cleared his mind and often allowed him to receive the solution needed to help cure a patient.

- We know that Albert Einstein used the technique of "sleeping." We are told he would work on a problem until he had exhausted all of his left-brain possibilities, then go to sleep. Sometimes during sleep the solution would appear in the form of a dream.

- Returning to nature enhances our creativity. Research at the University of Kansas disclosed that simple walks in nature heightened creativity and excursions, such as two or more days backpacking, can boost creativity by as much as 50 percent.

- My favorite is the process used by Thomas Edison. He would work and work on a problem and when no solution arrived, he then employed a fascinating technique. After he ate lunch, he would place a large metal bowl on his lap. Then, in his right hand he would hold two metal ball bearings over the metal bowl and allow himself to fall asleep. Of course, as he fell asleep, his hand would relax, releasing the metal balls. They would clang loudly as they fell into the metal bowl and awaken him. It was in that split second, in that state where he went from sleeping to being awakened, when he would sometimes receive the solution he had been unable to discover using his left-brain thinking.

- Another practical technique is utilized by

Randy Emelo, CEO of the highly successful Triple Creek organization, which focuses primarily on training and leadership development. For him, after jogging long and hard, followed by a hot shower, he says his creativity output is more productive than at any other time of the day.

*The key here is to remember you are looking for anything that shifts your focus. Everyone is different, so find the technique or practice that works best for you.*

I have recently discovered that my own creativity is especially strong in the morning, when I first wake up and my mind is suspended between sleep and being awake. All I have to do is bring to mind whatever book I am currently writing and I am usually given additional input to use. I have also learned that when the new information comes, I must immediately arise to write it down.

Of course, as with most writers, creativity flows the most during the actual writing process. For example, unlike most authors who type their manuscript, I still write my first draft with pencil and paper. When writing, I find that the hand holding the pencil suddenly takes off writing as fast as my hand can move, as it is fed information. Every once in a while I stop and ask myself where the information I've received came from because only seconds before I did not have that information.

Now, this is what happens to me and certainly you may have a totally different experience. But whatever you do, simply find the techniques that help you make the shift from left to right brain to get your creative juices flowing.

* * *

Here are some simple exercises that may help to stimulate those creative juices as well as disclose to you just how easy creativity can be applied in most any situation.

This first exercise is a simple one to discover how many uses you can imagine for an ordinary paperclip. Before you read further, brainstorm by yourself first—think of as many uses as you can conjure up.

Now, let's see if you came up with some of the following uses that I identified during my own brainstorming session (hopefully, you've come up with many, many more): If you were stranded in the wilderness, you could use the paperclip as a fish hook; it could be a fingernail cleaner; something to temporarily repair your glasses by holding the frames together; a key ring; a tool to pick a lock or scratch the inside of your ear, although your ear doctor would veto this idea. These are just a few of the innumerable uses one can find for a simple paperclip.

As a second exercise, take a bar of lead and consider it. I know the commodity price of metals has been soaring, but let's say a bar of lead has a price of $9. The question is *"How could we enhance the value of that lead bar?"* If we converted that bar into fish hooks, maybe its value would grow to $26; nails—$58; needles—$150; mechanisms used inside of a watch—$5,000.

This same principle can be even more easily seen in the artist Van Gogh's painting of a chair: the value of the chair—$35; the value of the painting—$200 million. Creativity can enhance the value of things, whether it is economic value or such intrinsic values as better health or beauty.

I heard a fascinating story where creativity was used by a community that was experiencing teenage violence. In trying to discover the cause of the problem, a rather odd suggestion came forth. It was proposed that the community clean up a large, heavily polluted pond located in the center of town.

Logically, this made no sense in connection with

the violence, but for some inexplicable reason the town decided to do exactly that. To their shocking surprise, after the whole town participated in cleaning the pond, the teenage violence plummeted. The only explanation was that somehow the polluted pond contributed to polluted negative attitudes by the kids. Additionally, the townspeople discovered that they then had a wonderful place where they could go and reflect.

What is of further interest is that when the person who made the suggestion to clean up the pond was asked in retrospect where the idea had come from, her response was that she didn't know; it had just popped into her mind.

*Never forget that our most important mental talent is our ability to imagine what* **never existed before.**

**A quote from *ALICE IN WONDERLAND:***

*"There is no use trying," said Alice. "One can't believe in impossible things."*

*"I daresay you haven't had much practice," said the Queen. "When I was your age, I always did it for half an hour a day. Why, sometimes I've believed in as many as six impossible things before breakfast."*

--Lewis Carroll (1832-1898)
English Author

# CHAPTER 7
## CREATIVITY, IT CAN BE USED EVERYWHERE

CREATIVITY CAN BE APPLIED TO ALL walks of life.

Way back at the turn of the 19th century, the Banner Creamery owners invested all their savings and every penny they could borrow to have a booth at the 1904 World's Fair held in St. Louis, Missouri. Their sales were going as planned until they erred by not ordering enough bowls in which to serve the ice cream. Remember, this was 1904 and you couldn't just go down to **Costco** and pick up thousands of paper or plastic bowls.

The owners, a couple with the last name of Band, were devastated. That night, they went home feeling completely hopeless. That is, until during the night and unable to sleep, one of them had a most creative thought. Waking the other, they arose and began to make waffles. Then, the wife "ironed" out the waffles, so they were very thin, and rolled them up while they were still hot. The next day they placed a scoop of ice cream on each cone and created the first ice cream cone in

America. They made a fortune.

Or what about Ivory soap? Here is a fable about how Ivory soap came to be.

The year was 1879 and Proctor & Gamble's bestselling products were candles and soap. But trouble appeared when Thomas Edison invented the light bulb. Seemingly overnight, candles became obsolete. Headed for bankruptcy, Proctor & Gamble's future looked bleak…until a forgetful employee at one of the company's factories in Ohio forgot to turn off his soap-making machine when he left for lunch. This brought about a huge mass of lather that filled with air bubbles. He was about to throw away his mess to hide the mistake, but because it was such a small mistake, he went ahead and poured the soap into frames for molding, then packaged the soap and sent them out.

A couple weeks later the company started to receive orders for more of that "floating soap."

I can still remember as a kid having great fun in the bathtub with Ivory's floating soap. But the reason why this was so important at the time was because most people bathed in the Ohio River and floating soap would not sink and be forever lost. It soon became a bestseller in Ohio and then spread to the rest of the country.

*The point is to never give up when things seemingly go wrong. Instead, use your creative mind to discover a solution.* ***In fact, this may be the very reason a dilemma has been presented to you—to show you an even better way.***

Guess what else? Another wonderful feature of creativity is that you're never too old to use it. Your body may be wearing out, but your creative mind never does. Remember these facts: Colonel Sanders was 65 when he started Kentucky Fried Chicken; Ray Croc of McDonald's hamburgers was 52; Amos Wallace, Jr. created Famous Amos Chocolate Chip Cookie Company when he was 41; Laura Ingalls Wilder was 65 when she began to write the *Little House on the Prairie* series; Golda Meir was 70 years old when she was elected as the fourth prime minister of Israel; and Grandma Moses was honored as Woman of the Year at age 88.

Do you need more proof?

The composer Verdi wrote "Ava Maria" at age 85; Pablo Casals played the cello and conducted orchestras until age 95; Michelangelo worked on sculptures until the day of his death at 89; Arthur Fiedler conducted the Boston Pops in his 80's; and Arthur Rubenstein was still playing the piano at 88.

***You're never too old to use creativity.*** There is

always a creative way to handle every situation you encounter in life. It's like the old farmer in Kansas who had a large pond on his land. One very hot afternoon, on the way to his pond, he grabbed a five-gallon bucket for the fruit he was about to pick. As he came nearer to the pond he heard some voices. Walking closer, he came upon a bunch of young women skinny-dipping. After making himself known to the women, they immediately went to the deep end of the pond and one woman yelled in his direction, "We're not coming out until you leave."

The old man paused a moment, all the while thinking he wouldn't mind seeing some naked young women, then held the bucket up and said, "Hey, I didn't come down here to watch you ladies swim naked in my pond. I came down here to feed the alligators."

Maybe creativity even improves with age. Who knows?

*"The world is but a canvas
to the imagination."*

--Henry David Thoreau (1817-1862)
Author, Poet and Philosopher

# CHAPTER 8
## HEALTH AND CREATIVITY

IN THE PRIOR CHAPTER YOU READ THAT Pablo Casals played the cello until the age of 95. But what you probably don't know is the incredible story disclosed when he was interviewed by Norman Cousins.

Norman Cousins was the man who cured himself of a rare and fatal blood disease by taking massive doses of Vitamin C and watching comedy movies every day during his healing period. He told his story in the book, *Anatomy of an Illness.*

Cousins had been trying for some time to get an interview with the famed artist. When the approval came, he was instructed to arrive at Casals' home not before 9:30 a.m., which he did. After waiting for the elderly musician, Cousins watched Pablo, who was crippled by arthritis, being assisted from his bedroom by his young wife, Marta. As Cousins walked up to the great man, he was told by Pablo that he would have to wait a minute.

This is where Cousins wrote that he saw a miracle unfold before his very eyes as he watched Pablo shuffle over to his piano—still with the help of his wife, and sit down. It was clear the man contended with an arthritic back, arms, and fingers. But, when he started to play the piano, Cousins said it was an image he would never forget. He observed that the playing began to loosen up Casals' crippled body.

Cousins said Casals started with a simple Mozart piece to warm up and ended with a very, very difficult Brahms Concerto. Finishing, he stood straight and erect and turned to Cousins. "Now we can do the interview."

Since the time I first read this story, I have done much research on the concept of creativity and healing and have discovered vast amounts of information verifying this connection.

The medical community confirms Casals' own experience that being creative and playing the piano can loosen up arthritic backs, arms, hands, and fingers. Hundreds of other examples are being discovered and the medical community has now acknowledged the power of the creative process as a healing force.

The latest medical findings more fully explain how art heals the body: it does so by changing a person's *attitude*, which then puts the person into a completely different brain wave pattern. This in turn affects the autonomous nervous system and brain neurotransmitters, which increases the blood flow to all the organs of the body and *changes the perception of pain.*

Now, you do not need to understand this physiological explanation. All you need to remember is that creativity can do phenomenal things to your mind and body. We are beginning to see that human life flows in the direction of creativity; it is your nature—it is who you really are—despite what others may have told you during your life; it is an overwhelming compulsion that must come out or you will experience a *blockage in your life that results in boredom and perhaps even disease.*

Creativity is proving to be one of the most powerful forces in the universe. Each of us was born with this inner power. Where some easily recognize it and use it in their lives, some of us, in a sense, are forced into using it only when confronted with difficult life problems.

**There does exist a definitive connection concerning the effects of creativity on our health.**

*"There is one thing stronger than all the armies in the world, and that is an idea whose time has come."*

--Victor Hugo (1802-1885)
French Novelist and Poet

# CHAPTER 9
## "HITTING THE WALL"

AS PROVOCATIVE AS IT MAY BE, THERE IS an identifiable step through which the creativity process operates.

Oddly enough, it is the part that no one wishes to talk about, the part no one wants to even acknowledge. As difficult as this step is, *though not always a requirement*, a creative solution often occurs **only** when you have exhausted every possibility; only when you have come to the detested conclusion that there is no answer to the problem; only when you *hit the wall* will the next step in the creativity process almost magically appear. The point is that you may actually need to go through the "agony of defeat" in order to get to the other side so that the solution can materialize. In these situations, you cannot skip over this arduous process in an attempt to get to the solution quicker; the *frustration* and *letting go* is **compulsory**.

We now at least acknowledge that many creative journeys begin with a dilemma of sorts and it is the *problem* that initiates the creative process. But what we have had difficulty fully comprehending is that this is sometimes the *pivotal point*; that it is only when we finally give up trying to find a solution, when we are overwhelmed with frustration and quit, that ironically provides the key to us finding the answer.

You see, we don't like admitting this part of our romantic tale as to how we persevered through all odds, through failure after failure, to finally succeed in breaking through the hidden blindness and find the perfect solution. We don't like to admit this because it might destroy the most popular notion of our story. Why? Because our society hates failure, and is embarrassed by it, despite the fact that it is through failure we learn the most.

This aspect in the creative process has been called such names as the *"aha" effect, insight, Eureka,* and an *epiphany*. These are psychological terms used to describe the process in problem-solving when a previously unsolvable puzzle or enigma becomes suddenly obvious and clear. One of the oldest and most cited examples of this came from a story involving the Greek scholar Archimedes.

The story goes that Archimedes was asked by a king if he could detect whether a crown was pure gold or if the goldsmith had added silver. Although he searched and searched for an answer, he was unable to do so until one day when he took a trip to one of the public baths. Out of the blue, he suddenly became aware that water was displaced every time someone's body sunk into the bath because the water level rose in the bath container. He next reasoned that the volume of water being displaced equaled the volume of the body being immersed. This meant that he could scientifically test the composition of a king's crown. Since gold is heavier than silver, pure gold would displace a greater volume of water than a mixture of gold and silver.

It was then that Archimedes was said to have jumped out of the public bath naked, ran home, all the while screaming "Eureka." He solved the problem but first had to go through being stuck; he had to reach an impasse before the solution arrived. Insights like this are believed to occur only when there has been a break in one's *mental fixation*, which then allows the solution to appear transparent and obvious.

Certainly, not all problems require such rigor. Most of our problems can be solved through left-brain logic. But for the really difficult problems—the ones where we give up out of frustration, where all of our hopes are dashed and completely obliterated—this difficult next step in the creative process will be required to lead us to the solution.

Now certainly, as I stated in the beginning, the more I write, the more frequently this creative state automatically appears and takes over my consciousness. It has become a habit; but it should be remembered that for the unique and really difficult problems life puts before us, the solution may first require us "hitting the wall."

Today, by using current medical machinery of MRI's and EEG's, we can discover what is immediately happening within the left brain. Obviously, when we are thinking intensely, these two machines of technology show great activity in the left-brain hemisphere. Conversely, when thinking has stopped and we have quit thinking in this side of our brain, the brain activity on the left side stops. Logical, right?

New research, however, has shown us something quite stunning; that when the left brain stops thinking, the right brain activity *increases*. This means that "hitting the wall," in not being able to find a solution and quitting, is the intangible act that shifts our thought processes to the right side where a whole new paradigm of thinking exists.

This may be hard to understand because it seems so illogical. See, we know that when one's arm is at rest the muscles in that arm are also at rest. But the two hemispheres of the brain act in opposition, meaning that when the left brain shuts down, the right brain activity takes over and offers realms of thinking not possible in the left side.

Remember the characteristics discussed earlier of the right brain? These include intuition, being in the *present*, our feeling side, spirituality, a sense of being interconnected, and a holistic way of viewing the world. These are characteristics that are *not* available in the left brain and are the amazing traits that allow us to view problems with a whole new criterion of thinking in the right hemisphere.

I can remember when I first began writing. Never having an inclination to do this before and having had no training, my insecurities were rampant. After finishing a prodigious number of rewrites and still sensing the book needed much more improvement, I came to a standstill and didn't know what to do next.

The solution came at a writers' meeting I had recently started to attend. Here someone shared that he improved his books by sending them out to people he either didn't know or people he knew who would be totally honest with their assessment. So I decided I would do this very same thing.

Well, the feedback from the first ten people devastated me, as only two or three thought my book, my *baby*, had any value at all. With this feedback and my insecurities, I slipped into a deep, three-day depression. Fortunately, as I emerged from the darkness, a little light bulb went on, carrying with it the idea that maybe it would be a good idea to incorporate some of the criticisms into changes to my book.

This eventually led to me to send out this revised book to ten new people for their criticisms. Lo and behold, this time I received six quite favorable responses and only four negative reviews.

What did I do next? I made new changes to reflect these negative criticisms and mailed them out to a book club consisting of thirteen members. This time I received twelve favorable comments with such statements as, "Who is this author?" and "Why haven't we ever heard of him before?"

As for the thirteenth member, she absolutely hated my book. I easily justified this by realizing that not even the famous author John Grisham would have received thirteen out of thirteen rave reviews.

This process worked so well for me, I now use

it with every new book I write. Though painful, it does produce better writing.

Think about this yourself. Can't you recall situations when you were unable to solve a problem and became so frustrated that you finally screamed out "to heck with it"? Then, after you thought you had totally and utterly let go of the damn problem and were on to some other line of thinking, suddenly, out of nowhere, the solution to the problem unexpectedly appeared? This is what I mean by "hitting the wall."

**Never forget: coming to the frustrating point where you can find no solution, where quitting seems your only option, may be the necessary next step needed for the solution to materialize.**

*"What is now proved
was once only imagined."*

--William Blake (1757-1827)
English Poet and Painter

# CHAPTER 10
## A MORE EFFECTIVE
## BRAINSTORMING METHOD

HERE IS THE ANSWER TO THE QUESTION I posed back in Chapter 1 regarding the newer, more effective "Brainstorming Method."

All my life, I have utilized the basic creative technique of *"brainstorming."* This was the process most used in corporations, businesses, schools, and organizations. Its rules were simple: a problem was posed; everyone participated; every idea was accepted no matter how far-fetched; criticism was taboo; and there was a time limit.

I must also admit that this system worked quite well and almost always produced new ideas beneficial to whatever organization I facilitated.

But one day while researching to see if there were advances made in the creative process, I was stunned when I came upon articles that proclaimed, "The Old Brainstorming Method Is Broken" and "Brainstorming Is No Longer the Optimum."

I have to admit my first glance at such absurd declarations caused every hackle on my body to rear up in defense of my old and trusted method.

That is, until I read over and over again that the *new brainstorming method* produced as much as **fifty percent more** *quality* **ideas** than the old system. This caught my attention and kept me reading.

Here are the two main differences between the old and new ways to brainstorm. The differences may seem quite small but do make a huge difference in generating beneficial new ideas:

1. The first difference is that rather than have the group come together to volunteer any and all ideas that pop up into anyone's mind, this newer approach starts with the individual, each person alone, brainstorming on a problem by *themselves*; and,

2. Second, after the individual brainstorming occurs, the next step is to have the individuals come together and share or pool their ideas. In this variation from the old approach to the new, the group is then asked to *critique each other's ideas.* In the old brainstorming method critiquing of any idea was off limits because of its tendency to stifle people from contributing their ideas. Paradoxically, the new method encourages conflict, and research has shown that individuals' egos can handle the criticism because…that the

## imagination is stronger than the ego!

You may be wondering that since these changes are rather small, how is it that the overall result is so significantly impacted? Again, studies have shown that the new brainstorming method produces *fifty percent* more quality creative ideas during the session, along with many other new ideas that trickle in over time.

One of the other discoveries made was that all the participating individuals had to be physically present to be effective. Why? It has become known that nonverbal communication may represent as much as 80 percent of the communication process. Therefore, brainstorming attempted via a conference call will never be as effective. People simply need to be present to see one another in order to be able to read each other's nonverbal clues.

I realize this new element of critiquing one another's ideas might seem counterintuitive, but it is correct; the reason being that it involves the dynamic processes of "debating" and "criticism." After individual brainstorming has taken place and the individuals are brought together into a group, the debating and criticizing of each individual's ideas actually *enhances* those ideas. Again, the surprising finding is that our egos can handle the criticisms, as long as the group as a whole is moving towards optimum solutions. Where we originally thought that non-criticism of ideas in the early stages was most effective for the creative process, this line of thinking has been proven to be *false*.

You've probably already concluded that this *new system* of generating creative ideas is not so much different than the old way, but let me emphasize again that although quite similar, the newly discovered little difference made a huge increase in creative idea output.

*"I have overcome many addictions during my life, but the one **drug** I cannot live without is **creativity**."*

--Ernie Carwile (1947-   )
American Author

# CHAPTER 11
## FEAR IS A WASTE OF TIME

The false myths that have been perpetuated by our world are alarming. As I mentioned earlier, one of those falsehoods is that we should never fail, never make mistakes. This idea exceeds the boundaries of absurdity because the real truth is that *failures* and *mistakes* are our greatest teachers.

I was leading a "growth group" back in the 80s. My agenda had been established and passed out to all the attendees, when I suddenly had an unsolicited idea come to mind. Out of the blue, I asked everyone to write down the three *best* things that had ever happened to them. Then another unsolicited idea popped into my mind and I asked them to write down the three *worst* events they'd encountered in life.

Interesting ideas, huh? But my next idea proved more profound: I asked them the simple little question, "Which did you learn the most from?"

Suddenly, the atmosphere in the room changed to a heavy stillness and no one said a thing, until finally a shy older woman asked the question that was on everyone's mind, "Does that mean the bad things that happen to us are really the best things?"

This question continues to obsess me some 30 years later, for I am reminded again and again that the difficult things that happen to us, the failures and errors, the things that our society looks down upon…are the exact things that teach us the most.

So, the next time you are held back in your creativity by your fear of failing, take a gander at these failures the world has produced, and never forget that your potential little failure, if it occurs, stands small in comparison.

## PAST WORLD *MISTAKES AND FALSE BELIEFS*

- The world is flat.
- The earth is the center of the solar system.
- The "philosopher's stone" could turn lead into gold and silver.
- We are all separate individuals.
- Money solves all problems.
- More is better.
- Animals are dumb beings.
- The brain communicates with the heart while the heart cannot communicate with the brain.
- If God wanted man to fly, He would have given him wings.

# Chapter 11

If the world once believed these falsehoods to be true, then we must question ourselves: **What do we now believe to be true that will be proven false in our very near future?**

*"If I have seen **within**, it is by standing on the shoulders of giants who came before me."*

--Isaac Newton (1642-1727)
English Physicists, Mathematician
and Astronomer

# CHAPTER 12
## WE MUST WORK TOGETHER

WHERE CREATIVITY HAS MOST CERTAINLY been present throughout history, its understanding and usage were often limited to just a few gifted individuals. This allowed people to be able to literally pick off new ideas like an apple from a tree.

As our world has grown increasingly more complex, the success of individual or solitary creativity must now move towards and focus more on *joint creativity*. Said differently, some of our world's problems are so complex that we must pool our imaginations in order to find solutions; we must use teamwork.

The genius Buckminster Fuller coined the term "synergy," which literally means that when two or more things function together they produce something that would have been impossible to produce independently. A simple example of human synergy is when two people are too short to reach an apple in a tree. One solution might be for one of the individuals to sit on the shoulder of the other in order to reach the apple. Here, the product of synergy is the acquisition of one apple.

Another of Einstein's quotes stands out and further augments the importance of us learning to work together: "Human beings have a kind of optical illusion; they see themselves as *separate* rather than a *part of the whole.*"

I believe that if we do not come to realize we are all together on this one ship called earth and that we must work in concert with each other, we will perish. No longer can we see ourselves as separate.

It's like the ancient Greek legend:

> *Several men traveled by boat from one Greek island to another. Men of higher rank sat in the rear, or stern of the boat—a place reserved for them. For the reasonable fare of two drachmas, they could sit there and enjoy a small but well-appointed cabin, while being safe from the elements. The poor, on the other hand, found themselves in the front, or bow, which was set on the opposite end from the rich boat travelers.*

> *A single drachma secured for these poor travelers a seat in the open front of the boat; there they suffered the indignity and discomfort of being soaked by the ocean spray that came over the bow,*

*were burned by the sun, and became drenched by the sudden showers that often occurred on the Aegean Sea.*

*On this particular day, though, the Aegean Sea was calm. A steady breeze filled the sails. The rich men were lounging inside the cabin, eating delicacies, such as the best olives and cheeses, and drinking only the finest wines available.*

*Suddenly, the bow sprang a leak. Water gushed up through the planks of the boat's deck, and within a few minutes it began to sink—bow first. The captain ran to the stern and cried to the first-class passengers, "We're sinking! Abandon ship!"*

*One of the men of rank, a wealthy Greek merchant, got up from the table and peered out of the cabin door. Upon seeing that it was only the bow that was nearly submerged, he turned to his comrades and confidently assured them, "Have no fear. It's only their end of the boat that's sinking."*

In my eighth book in this series ***And the Animals Shall Teach Us...Angels In Disguise***, I cite the fact that a flock of geese can fly something like 70% further than one individual goose alone. This one little truth might provide us all with the larger understanding that as one united world acting together, we too can fly much further, safer, and better.

**If we continue to believe that all of us exist separately from everything on this planet, we shall surely perish. This is proving to be very true in the area of creativity. To solve today's difficult problems, the pooling of ideas must be strongly encouraged and used whenever necessary.**

# CREATIVITY

*It strikes like lighting,*
*Illuminating the mind,*
*Providing hope,*
*A spark of Divine.*

*This new idea feels certain,*
*How did it arise?*
*It came from where?*
*I suddenly feel wise.*

*But how can I own it?*
*Though I argue it's from me.*
*Yet the truth of the matter,*
*It's from somewhere I cannot see.*

*In an instant of a second,*
*It somehow appeared.*
*I'm ensconced in a feeling,*
*Of wisdom far beyond my years.*

*The solution now uncovered,*
*I take the credit.*

*But deep, deep inside me,*
*I know better.*

*This invisible force,*
*Surrounds me everywhere.*
*All I need do,*
*Is request it to appear.*

*"Imagination rules the world."*

--Napoleon Bonaparte (1769-1821)
French Military and Political Leader

# CHAPTER 13
## USING CREATIVITY TO SOLVE EVERYDAY PROBLEMS

I WANT TO EMPHASIZE AGAIN THAT creativity is applicable to *every facet of life*, not only with business problems or in the arena of fine arts, such as music, acting, painting, sculpting, and writing. Creativity can be utilized in every aspect of one's life: cooking, arranging furniture and flowers, strengthening friendships and relationships with children, spouses, and other family members, establishing household budgets, and aiding in the establishment of balance in one's time between work and play—**everywhere**.

Here are a couple of instances where I used creativity in my own life:

My daughter went through a short phase of hitting and spitting on her friends. My talks with her about it did no good whatsoever, something quite unusual since reasoning with her normally worked. One day when I saw her hit one of her friends, I ran up to spank her. But just before I did, the thought ran through my mind that there was something *absurd* about hitting my child in an attempt to get her to stop hitting others. I needed to be creative and come up with a much better response. I needed some more choices, better options in how to respond; so I called a friend who was a psychologist and asked him what I should do.

His solution was simple. He asked me what her buttons was—what **toy** did she hold dearest to her heart? I knew immediately it was her **stuffed rabbit**—her "Bunny Two-Shoes." Then he suggested I inform her that I was going to take away her precious toy for a while if she ever hit someone again.

There was no question that her stuffed bunny was her tried and true security object. So, the next time she hit someone, I walked her and her bunny up to the linen closet, took away her bunny, placed it in the closet and closed its door.

Well, the result was as if I had physically harmed her. She fell down crying in a most dramatic and theatrical way and begged to have her Bunny Two-Shoes back. After only 60 seconds or so, I opened up the closet door, returned the bunny to the poor sobbing little waif, and guess what? Her hitting and spitting behavior stopped, permanently.

Next, I had a problem neighbor who was just downright mean and angry at me for something I could never figure out. One day I came to the end of my patience when I saw that this ninny had heaved a huge rock over our adjoining fence into my yard. I saw *red* and began scheming how I would not only get even, but intended to do much, much greater harm to him.

Fortunately, a wise friend of mine interrupted my planning with a telephone call. Angrily, I explained the horrible thing my problem neighbor had done most recently and then began to share some of the childish ploys I was considering to punish my evil neighbor.

After running through all of the possibilities, my friend said nothing until I foolishly asked him for his opinion. From the silence over the telephone I knew he was thinking. When he finally spoke, his new proposal initially stunned me, but then shook up my frame of reference enough for me to see another possibility. He suggested I knock on the man's door and thank him for giving me the big rock. "Explain to him that you had just decided to create a *rock garden* in your backyard and the man's big rock would be the centerpiece."

I had to calm down before I did it, but the results were amazing. I could tell from my neighbor's facial expression that at first he was ready to fight with me. When I finished thanking him, his jaw first fell open, then he kind of smiled, and though confused, told me I was welcome.

I never had a problem with him after that. Although we never became friends, we at least were able to greet each other when our paths crossed. And the rock garden, it stayed in my backyard until I sold the house. It continues to remind me there are always different ways to skin a cat.

You see, when faced with a problem, most of us seem to have only one or two options to choose from. The point is that ***creativity can increase those options.*** One no longer has to be limited with just a few possibilities, but can draw on a large menu from which to make a selection, one that might even be a win-win solution for everyone involved.

It is easy to use creativity; all you have to do is identify the problem and then ask yourself, "What is the best solution?" Your answer may come quickly, or you may have to resort to using one of the techniques for shifting from the "left" side of the brain to the "right" side. No matter which technique you use, you can find the right solution.

*"If everyone is thinking alike,
then someone isn't thinking."*

--Gen. George S. Patton (1885-1945)
U. S. General during World War II

# CHAPTER 14
# RETICULAR ACTIVATION SYSTEM (RAS)

THERE ARE TWO FINAL IDEAS I WOULD like to bring to your attention.

The first idea is definitely negative, but one that must be addressed, though only lightly. One of my early reviewers challenged me when he asked, "Can't creativity also be used for evil?"

The answer to this uncomfortable question is yes. And like everything in life, we humans have the option of using these principles for good or evil. This is simply a choice each of us must make individually.

The second idea is definitely encouraging; located in the brain stem of every human is the "reticular activating system," or RAS. While the RAS has many functions, perhaps the most important function is its control of consciousness, our ability to consciously focus attention on something. It also acts as a filter, dampening the effect of such repeated stimuli as loud noises, lessening the effect of all the enormous data our senses pick up. This helps prevent our senses from overloading. It's the reason we aren't overwhelmed by the vast amount of sensory stimuli that constantly bombards us.

The most fascinating element of the RAS is that it reveals to us the stuff we want to see, the stuff that is foremost in our thinking and blocks out what we aren't interested in. For example, if you buy a new **Hyundai car**, you surprisingly start seeing Hyundais wherever you drive. If you're pregnant, you begin to notice all the pregnant women who enter your environment.

It has been strongly emphasized that we attract what we think about. If you believe this little maxim, it doesn't take a rocket scientist to bridge its applicability to our lives and the role the RAS plays. If you do not like what is in your life, change what you are bringing into your thoughts.

The same is true about creativity. If you want to have more creativity in your life, then remember to use it. Simply identify the problem and then ask yourself, "What is the best solution?"

*"Creativity is to life,
as spice is to food."*

--Maxwell Winston Stone

# CONCLUSION

*I HAVE JUST WRITTEN THE LAST WORDS IN my creativity book. Feeling grand and fulfilled, perhaps not much different than a mother who has given birth, I sense I am in a state of grace and hope this feeling will remain.*

*But within days, my old negative feelings of restlessness and irritability return. Entering the kitchen, I fill a bowl with my favorite ice cream, **Blue Bell's** latest creation of Rocky Mountain Road. Ice cream often cures my ills. This time it doesn't. I pace the floor and scan my consciousness for some clue as to why I am feeling awry, but intuit nothing.*

*As a last resort, I return to my desk and absentmindedly pick up a pencil and begin doodling on a piece of paper until the doodling progresses to writing. Before I am aware of what I'm doing, I find myself beginning another book; this time a fictional story; gold, lost treasure, and past lives enter my imagination.*

*Unconsciously, the invisible Source connects with my mind and words begin to flow. I do not know where it comes from—only that it inhabits me and I find that my hand begins to move involuntarily and I am once again transported to the holy...*

✳ ✳ ✳

**My hope is that this little book will stir your creativity so that you will utilize it in all of your affairs.**

# ABOUT THE AUTHOR

ERNIE CARWILE WAS BORN IN MUNICH, Germany and has lived throughout the world. He is a graduate of the University of Missouri and the Iliff School of Theology in Denver, Colorado.

After high school he sold cemetery plots door-to-door in Hannibal, Missouri, and while attending college, he drove one of the huge trucks for Peabody Coal Mine. Mr. Carwile has been an Air force Officer, heavyweight boxer and a Methodist and Congregational minister.

As a celebrated author and master storyteller, Carwile has been featured extensively in the national media including *Good Morning America, Inside Edition, CNN, Associated Press, Court TV, Clear Channel Radio, the Los Angeles Time and the Rocky Mountain News.*

His books have received a great review from the most prestigious **Library Journal**, as well as Endorsements/Thank You's from the **President of the United States, twelve U.S. Governors and such prominent collegiate football coaches as**

**Steve Spurrier.**

They also have been translated into **five foreign languages.**

This is his ninth book in the Maxwell Winstone Stone Series, a fifteen book series.